Take Control of Your Credit Today!

By Adam Richards

First Printing: 2017

ISBN 978-1-387-35900-4

www.cleanupyourcreditreport.com

TABLE OF CONTENTS

ANYONE CAN DO IT

Have you ever found yourself wondering why everyone else seems to have the financial freedom to buy things that you can't even afford to dream about? The truth is, there's a very good chance that they are funding their dreams with credit. Even the rich and famous bank their cash and use plastic to pay. The part of "The American Dream" that people don't talk about is, that it is brought to you by American Express.

Credit can be like a dangerous game of Russian Roulette, one false step and your FICO score takes one to the head. Because I grew up in a wealthy family, I never really paid attention until it was too late. By then, I had a stack of unpaid hospital bills, defaulted credit cards and a slew of charge-offs. It had become one of those things that I was just too ashamed to deal with. You learn to operate on cash and live with less. Nowadays, I have a regular monthly income, and I've learned to be responsible with the minimal debt I am able to incur, and I'm doing okay, but really, this nickel and dime stuff is for the birds!

Fixing my credit seemed like a long shot and an expensive proposition until one day I started doing some research and found about a million books on Amazon HOW TO FIX MY CREDIT IN JUST 90 DAYS!!! All I had to do was shell out some cash and I would be good to go! If you are reading this, that's was what you were thinking, or hoping, right? Ahh, Capitalism at it's best. People are making money on some secret trick, and according to several of the titles in my queue, it has something to do with the number 609.

Turns out, 609 is a loophole in The Fair Reporting Act that says that anything listed on a person's credit report must be verified by the physical verification of a signed contract. In other words, for every account listed on your report, the reporting agency must have a hard copy of your signed commitment to receive credit for services rendered and to pay it back under the agreed upon terms on file. The Big Three - Equifax, Experion and Trans-Union do EVERYTHING electronically, and understandably so. Imagine the acres of warehouses it would take just to store one signed contract for every account for every person in the civilized world. Now imagine the manpower it would take. Yeah, that's just not happening.

So that's it, right there. That is the key to taking control of your credit. In the following pages I will show you how to use this loophole to have negative items on your credit report removed which will in turn up your FICO score, which will up your credit. Let me tell you from the start, it is not hard to do, but it is tedious and time consuming and requires organization and commitment. It's also inexpensive and usually takes only 30 days or so to see some results, but like most things in life, the more time and effort you put in to it the more results you will see. My goal here is to make it as easy as possible for you to jump right in. I can't say it enough, patience and tenacity pay big in this game. The Big Three are not there to make your life easier, but, they DO have to obey the law and WILL eventually respond to the squeaky wheel approach.

I am not a guy who wants a big house and a boat, I just want to have what I need every day and help others along the way. That's why even though much of the information is the same as is contained in the more expensive How-To books, I want to make it affordable and accessible to people for whom a little credit goes a long way. People like me.

Your FICO® Score helps lenders make accurate, reliable and fast credit risk decisions across the customer lifecycle based on credit reports from The Big Three. The credit risk score rank-orders consumers by how likely they are to pay their credit obligations as agreed.

KNOWLEDGE IS POWER

I mentioned earlier that the process of cleaning up your credit report is not expensive, really, all you have to pay for is Certified Postage, assuming that you have access to a computer and printer. You are playing with the big boys now so you want to be stupidly professional and organized. For myself, I like a hard copy of everything, so I set up a simple 3-folder system, each one designated with one the names of The Big Three. You can just as easily do that on your computer's desktop. At this writing, a first class stamp is 49 cents and sending it Certified Mail costs $3.35. That come to just over $10 for one round of letters, the most it usually takes is four rounds; one mailing every 30 days - just to give you a ballpark depending how far you go with it and if you choose to send additional correspondence for specific line entries.

Obviously, having a computer and printer makes things much easier. You will need a word processor program. If you don't have MS WORD, or something similar, you may want to try openoffice.org and download their FREE like-Word office suite. You will also want to insert a pic or scan of your license and Social Security card into the DEMAND LETTERS. If you don't have Adobe Photoshop, or something like it, you may need to get creative. I took pics and cropped them with my phone and then emailed them to my MacBook, downloaded them and inserted them in the word processor. I realize that this kind of thing may seem over the top, and I will explain later why it's not, but it is what I warned you about earlier about being meticulous and patient. I want to lay it all out before you start so that you know what you are getting yourself in to. I am the king of impatience, but I'm pretty sure that a little investment of my time now could make for a much brighter future.

The first step is to know and understand what you are dealing with. You can get a free yearly credit report from The Big Three at www.anualcreditreport.com. If for some reason you are unable to obtain all three, getting just one of them will get the ball rolling. Equifax, Experion and Trans-Union contain about 80-90% of the same information, so what you don't catch on this round you can catch on the next. You will receive a copy of your credit report with their response to you Demand Letter. Any missing entries can just be added to the next mailing. Now it's time to look the credit monster in the eye. Don't be surprised by what you may see!

Myth: Shopping around for a loan hurts your score.
Fact: It is true that too many inquires to your credit will
lower your score. It is very common to see anywhere from
3-5 points deducted from your credit score for each hard
inquiry. Scores range from 300-800 so impact is minimal.

Your Credit Report & You

Once you have a credit report, take a few minutes to look it over. They are presented in a fairly simple format. Once I understood what I was looking at it took away the mystery and made me feel, for the first time, that maybe this is something I can actually do.

Identify all of the negative entries. If there are few or none that make you look good, you can see why it is suggested that you obtain some kind of secured credit card so that there is something positive for creditors to look at. As mentioned earlier, you will want to list EVERYTHING in your first Demand Letter, including student loans, car loans, or anything that makes you look less than reliable. If there are accounts still open, list them, but you may also want to consider sending a Letter of Goodwill to those individuals. Remember, if there is no original contract collecting dust in the Credit Reporting Agencies archives, any and all accounts listed are eligible to be challenged. Since there may be issues reported by one of The Big Three and not the other. It is well worth your time create a master list to keep track. Don't give them an opportunity to find a loophole in YOUR record keeping

The FICO Pie

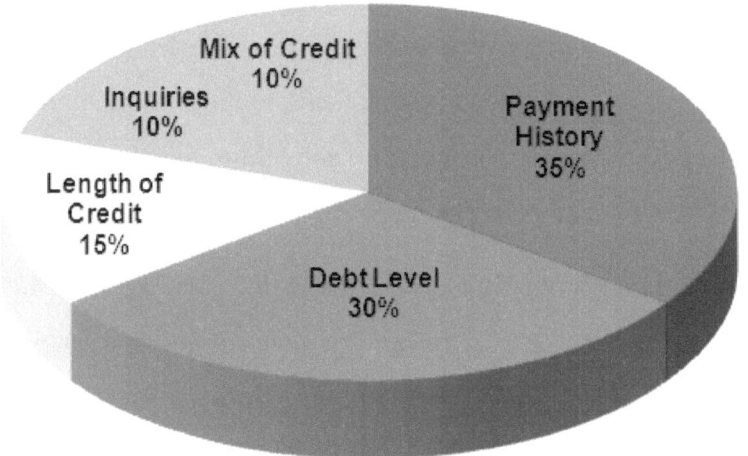

ROUND ONE: Put Up Your Dukes

Now that you have all of the information that you need to get started, it's time to put together DEMAND LETTER #1. You will want your wording to be direct and concise. You can see a fully completed sample letter at the end, in the meantime, the wording goes something like this:

According to the Fair Credit Reporting Act, **Section 609 (a)(1)(A)**, *you are required by federal law to verify* - *through the physical verification of the original signed consumer contract - any and all accounts you post on a credit report. Otherwise, anyone paying for your reporting services could fax, mail or email in a fraudulent account.*

*I demand to see Verifiable Proof (**an original Consumer Contract with my Signature on it**) you have on file of the accounts listed below. Your failure to positively verify these accounts has hurt my ability to obtain credit. Under the FCRA, unverified accounts must be removed and if you are unable to provide me a copy of verifiable proof, you must remove the accounts listed below.*

Using your MASTER LIST, you want to include ALL of the negative entries on your credit report identifying each account with the exact name of the creditor/collections listed, and an account number. You won't have access to the whole number, usually just the last four digits, but include all the x's, if it is listed at all. Each account should be a separate line item. Using your word processor's table function is probably your best bet, check out the example below. The more clear and concise, the better!

Account listing example:

Name of Account	Account Number	Verification Status
Verizon Wireless	xxxxxxxxxxx67407	Unverified Account
Trident Assets	xxxxxxxx6665100	Unverified Account
Apex Asset Mgt	xxxxxx778	Unverified Account
Apex Asset Mgt	xxxxxx846	Unverified Account
Apex Asset Mgt	xxxxxx345	Unverified Account
Apex Asset Mgt	xxxxxx098	Unverified Account
Apex Asset Mgt	xxxxxx867	Unverified Account
Apex Asset Mgt	xxxxxx672	Unverified Account
AR Resources LTD	xxxxxxxxxxxxx6773	Unverified Account
National Recovery	xxxxxxx7836	Unverified Account

After you have made sure that everything is filled in correctly, you will need to get you letters notarized. The Big Three will use any and every excuse in the book to disqualify your dispute. Don't give them ammunition. Having your letters notarized will give you legal verification and documentation of both the letter itself and the integrity of it's content.

I would also suggest including, *a request to remove all non-account holding inquiries over 30 days old.* This will minimize the impact of credit report inquiries, of which you will notice on your report, there are two types. The first is a "Soft Query" that provides a summary overview of your credit history, whereas a "Hard Query" is a pulling of your whole credit report, and that's the one that has the most negative impact. A lender sees a bunch of inquiries but no corresponding account which tells him that you were not approved and is another strike against you.

One of the standard first responses is to question the authenticity of the request and the sender, rendering a decision to take no action because the correspondence is deemed invalid. Scanning an image of your Social Security card and Driver's License/State ID into the document is another pre-strike against the administrative shenanigans intended to discourage and sidetrack you. You may still get the form letter, but it another weapon in your future arsenal. Also depending on the length of your letter, printing front and back prevents any "loss" of pages.

A quick note about getting your letters notarized. Unless you know someone who has a commission, places like FedEx and The UPS Store charge up to $15.00 per signature. However, if you have a bank account, your bank will do it for free. Sometimes it takes going to another branch, but it's well worth the savings to make some calls ahead. To keep it professional, it's a good idea to add the standard notary form to the end of your letter.

Standard Notary Public documentation form:

STATE OF:
COUNTY OF:

I HEREBY CERTIFY that on this day before me, an officer duly qualified to take acknowledgments, personally appeared
_____, who is personally known to me or who has produced _____ as identification and who executed the foregoing instrument and he/she acknowledged before me that he/she executed the same.

WITNESS my hand and official seal

in the County and State aforesaid this _____ day of
_____ 2017.

_____

Notary Public Signature

_____

Printed Name: _____

My commission expires: _____

Lastly, sending your letters CERTIFIED MAIL is an

important part of protecting yourself and preventing "loss."

For an additional $6 you can add Return Receipt Service, which will give you a recipient name, but all you really need is proof of delivery. Having a name would only come in handy if you have exhausted all your options and decide to instigate legal action. More about that later. So everything is in the mail and now you wait...

The Big Three Update Their Reporting Every 30 Days.
If you want it to happen quicker, you can ask a Mortgage
Loan Officer, in the interests of purchasing a home in the
near future, to do a RAPID RESCORE so that you can have
the most current information while shopping for loans.
Heck, everyone wants to buy a house someday!

What's Next

Probably the first thing you will receive from The Big Three is confirmation that the Promotional Suppression has been placed on your account. From there, Credit Reporting Agencies are required by law to respond to disputes in 30 days. And there is a good chance that they will try to blow you off with some lame excuse or technicality. Or it may take a couple of rounds of letters to get a response. Don't lose hope! You have the law on your side. If they are reporting it and don't have a hardcopy signed document they are NOT ALLOWED to report it. Statue 609 is very clear and in place for a reason: anyone can transmit information, true or false, to the CRA's. You are just demanding that before they mess with your credit score, they verify the information. So don't let them distract you with any other response than, "THE ACCOUNT HAS BEEN REMOVED."

Just a small heads-up, they may try to detour your dispute with alternate ways of resolving issue, but letters like these ARE the time-proven method. Using an online grievance system leaves you without the paper trail that could win your case. Don't let them distract you! As I mentioned earlier, contained with their response from your first letter will be an updated Credit Report. Hopefully your first correspondence did something to clean things up. At this point, whatever is still there needs to be worked on from both angles: The Big Three and the reporting debtor/collection   agency.

For any accounts still open, you will want to send a Letter of Goodwill. This is basically a letter trying to convince your creditor to allow you to get back on track and to lay-off on the bad credit reporting. (see SAMPLE LETTERS – Letter of Goodwill)

All other debtors/collection agencies should be sent a letter of VALIDATION. This is a document that states that a service was rendered, what the service was, and the cost for each service involved. They may try to provide VERIFCATION, but this is not what The Law requires. (see SAMPLE LETTERS – Request for Validation)

Hopefully whomever is reviewing your case will be in a generous mood, but probably not. Don't be discouraged if your first letter doesn't move mountains – you still have three more to go, and then you can start threatening legal actions, that's when they really get squirrely. For example, medical collections accounts for over 43% of bad credit, mostly because this industry has no other recourse. It's not like they are gonna re-break your arm. What's interesting about MEDICAL CASES is that because of HIPPA (Health Insurance Privacy and Accountability Act), healthcare providers are not allowed to share your information without your signed consent, but in order for the credit agencies to legally validate the debt, they have to have documentation that your doctor can't legally provide without a HIPPA RELEASE and chances are, he didn't have you sign any waivers for collection agencies when you were having your wisdom tooth removed. (see Sample Letters – HIPPA VIOLATION)

Mail Round #2 of letters 30 days after you have confirmed receipt of letter number one, which can easily be done with online with the Certified Mail tracking number at www.usps.com. If you want to wait a few extra days for any replies that haven't come in yet, I wouldn't go more than a week. Keep in mind, they might not answer at all, so don't give up. Keep poking the bear. Ideally, you will have your responses in hand and you can make any necessary adjustments to Demand Letter #2 by day 30. Either way, you will want to get any Letters of Goodwill and/or Requests for Validation out in the mail as soon as possible. Same with rounds three and four.

If at that point you want to keep hacking away at anything left, you have the option of taking legal steps. This is potentially costly and makes the process that I just described look like child's play. However, if you decide to go the legal route you can get all the information you need at: www.ftccomplaintassistant.

As we said at the beginning, the more time and effort you put in to it, the more successful you will be. It definitely bares repeating, the law is on your side, demanding that big companies and debit collectors follow it is a service to everyone. I wish you good luck and the wisdom to make smart decisions with your new credit scores!

Once you get it back – Keep it! Keep balances low on credit cards and other "revolving credit". High outstanding debt can affect a credit score. Pay off debt rather than moving it around. The most effective way to improve your credit scores in this area is by paying down your revolving (credit cards) debt.

RESOURCES

Equifax
P.O. Box 740256 Atlanta, GA 30374-0256

Experian

P.O. Box 4500 Allen, TX 75013

Trans Union
P.O. Box # 2000 Chester, PA. 19022-2000

FICO Score

www.myfico.com

Free Credit Report

www.annualcreditreport.com

Free Word Processing Software

www.openoffice.org/download/

Free Photo Editing Software:

www.getpaint.net/index.html/

5 TOP WAYS TO BUILD YOUR CREDIT

- Apply for a secured credit card. It is the universally agreed BEST way to build credit.
- Apply for a credit-builder loan.
- Get a co-signer.
- Become an authorized user on someone else's credit card. .
- Get credit for the rent you pay

SAMPLE LETTERS

As you can see, with each mailing, the wording gets stronger. You can use similar verbiage following up with collection agency correspondence.

DEMAND LETTER #1 – Sample

According to the Fair Credit Reporting Act, **Section 609 (a)(1)(A), you are required by federal law to verify** - through the physical verification of the original signed consumer contract - any and all accounts you post on a credit report. Otherwise, anyone paying for your reporting services could fax, mail or email in a fraudulent account.

I demand to see Verifiable Proof (**an original Consumer Contract with my Signature on it**) you have on file of the accounts listed below. Your failure to positively verify these accounts has hurt my ability to obtain credit. Under the FCRA, unverified accounts must be removed and if you are unable to provide me a copy of verifiable proof, you must remove the accounts listed below. **I am demanding the following accounts be verified or removed immediately.**

Name of Account	Account Number	Verification Status
Verizon Wireless	xxxxxxxxxxx67407	Unverified Account
Trident Assets	xxxxxxxx6665100	Unverified Account
Advanced Collections	xxxxx4566	Unverified Account
Receivable Mgt	xxx3495	Unverified Account
Receivable Mgt	xxx8993	Unverified Account
Receivable Mgt	xxx7609	Unverified Account
Apex Asset Mgt	xxxxxx778	Unverified Account

DEMAND LETTER #2 – Sample

Please be advised this is my SECOND WRITTEN REQUEST. The unverified items listed below remain on my credit report in violation of Federal Law. You are required under the FCRA to have a copy of the original creditors documentation on file to verify that this information is mine and is correct. In the results of your first investigation, you stated in writing that you **"verified"** that these items are being **"reported correctly"** ? Who verified these accounts?

You have **NOT** provided me a copy of ANY original documentation required under **Section 609 (a)(1)(A) & Section 611 (a)(1)(A)** (a consumer contract with my signature on it) and under **Section 611 (5)(A)** of the FCRA – you are required to *"...promptly DELETE all information which cannot be verified."*

The law is very clear as to the Civil liability and the remedy available to me for "negligent noncompliance" (**Section 617**) if you fail to comply. **I am a litigious consumer and fully intend on pursuing litigation in this matter to enforce my rights under the FCRA. I demand the following accounts be verified or deleted immediately.**

Name of Account	Account Number	Verification Status
Verizon Wireless	xxxxxxxxxxx67407	Unverified Account
Trident Assets	xxxxxxxx6665100	Unverified Account
Advanced Collections	xxxxx4566	Unverified Account
Apex Asset Mgt	xxxxxx778	Unverified Account

Please remove all **non-account holding inquiries** over 30 days old.

DEMAND LETTER #3 – Sample

Please be advised this is my THIRD WRITTEN REQUEST and FINAL WARNING that I fully intend to pursue litigation in accordance with the FCRA to enforce my rights and seek relief and recover all monetary damages that I may be entitled to under Section 616 and Section 617 regarding your continued willful and negligent noncompliance.

Despite two written requests, the unverified items listed below still remain on my credit report in violation of Federal Law. You are required under the FCRA to have a copy of the original creditors documentation on file to verify that this information is mine and is correct. In the results of your first investigation and subsequent reinvestigation, you stated in writing that you **"verified"** that these items are being **"reported correctly"?** Who verified these accounts? You have **NOT** provided me a copy of ANY original documentation (a consumer contract with my signature on it) as required under **Section 609 (a)(1)(A) & Section 611 (a)(1)(A).** Furthermore you have failed to provide the method of verification as required under **Section 611 (a) (7)**. Please be advised that under **Section 611 (5)(A)** of the FCRA – you are required to *"...promptly DELETE **all information which cannot be verified."***

The law is very clear as to the Civil liability and the remedy available to me (**Section 616 & 617**) if you fail to comply with Federal Law. I am a litigious consumer and fully intend on pursuing litigation in this matter to enforce my rights under the FCRA.

I demand the following accounts be verified or deleted immediately:

Name of Account	Account Number	Verification Status
Verizon Wireless	xxxxxxxxxxx67407	Unverified Account
Trident Assets	xxxxxxxx6665100	Unverified Account
Advanced Collections	xxxxx4566	Unverified Account
Apex Asset Mgt	xxxxxx778	Unverified Account
Apex Asset Mgt	xxxxxx846	Unverified Account
Apex Asset Mgt	xxxxxx345	Unverified Accountß
Apex Asset Mgt	xxxxxx098	Unverified Account
Apex Asset Mgt	xxxxxx867	Unverified Account
Apex Asset Mgt	xxxxxx672	Unverified Account
National Recovery	xxxxxxx7836	Unverified Account

Please remove all **non-account holding inquiries** over 30 days old.

Please add a **Promotional Suppression** to my credit file.

DEMAND LETTER #4 – Sample

<u>NOTICE OF PENDING LITIGATION SEEKING RELIEF AND MONETARY DAMAGES UNDER FCRA SECTION 616 & SECTION 617</u>

Please accept this final written OFFER OF SETTLEMENT BEFORE LITIGATION as my attempt to amicably resolve your continued violation of the Fair Credit Reporting Act regarding your refusal to delete UNVERIFIED information from my consumer file. I intend to pursue litigation in accordance with the FCRA to seek relief and recover all monetary damages that I may be entitled to under Section 616 and Section 617 if the UNVERIFIED items listed below are not deleted immediately. A copy of this letter as well as copies of the three written letters sent to you previously will also become part of a formal complaint to the Federal Trade Commission and shall be used as evidence in pending litigation provided you fail to comply with this offer of settlement.

Despite three written requests, the unverified items listed below still remain on my credit report in violation of Federal Law. You are required under the FCRA to have a copy of the original creditors documentation on file to verify that this information is mine and is correct. In the results of your investigations, you stated in writing that you **"verified"** that these items are being **"reported correctly"?** Who verified these accounts? You have **NOT** provided me a copy of ANY original documentation (a consumer contract with my signature on it) as required under **Section 609 (a)(1)(A) & Section 611 (a)(1)(A).** Furthermore you have failed to provide the method of verification as required under **Section 611 (a) (7)**. Please be advised that under **Section 611 (5)(A)** of the FCRA – you are required to *"...promptly DELETE all information which cannot be verified."*

The law is very clear as to the Civil liability and the remedy available to me (**Section 616 & 617**) if you fail to comply with Federal Law. I am a litigious consumer and fully intend on pursuing litigation in this matter to enforce my rights under the FCRA.

I demand the following accounts be verified or deleted immediately

Please remove all **non-account holding inquiries** over 30 days old. Please add a **Promotional Suppression** to my credit file.

Name of Account	Account Number	Verification Status
Verizon Wireless	xxxxxxxxxxx67407	Unverified Account
Trident Assets	xxxxxxxx6665100	Unverified Account
Apex Asset Mgt	xxxxxx778	Unverified Account
Apex Asset Mgt	xxxxxx846	Unverified Account
Apex Asset Mgt	xxxxxx345	Unverified Accountß
Apex Asset Mgt	xxxxxx098	Unverified Account
Apex Asset Mgt	xxxxxx867	Unverified Account
Apex Asset Mgt	xxxxxx672	Unverified Account
AR Resources LTD	xxxxxxxxxxxxx6773	Unverified Account
National Recovery	xxxxxxx7836	Unverified Account

REQUEST FOR VALIDATION – Sample Letter

This letter is being sent to you in response to notices sent to me from your company and more importantly, due to your erroneous reporting to the Credit Bureau(s), the negative impact on my personal credit report. Please be advised that this is not a refusal to pay, but a notice sent pursuant to the Fair Debt Collection Practices Act, 15 USC 1692g Sec. 809 {b} that your claim is disputed and validation is requested.

This is NOT a request for "verification" or proof of my mailing address, but a request for VALIDATION made pursuant to the above named Title and Section. I respectfully request that your offices provide me with competent evidence that I have any legal obligation to pay you.

Please provide the following:

- What services or products am I being charged for
- Explain and show me calculations used to derive the balance
- Provide me with copies of any papers that show I agreed to pay what you say I owe
- Provide a verification or copy of any judgment, if applicable
- Identify the original creditor and point of purchase
- Prove the Statute of Limitations has not expired on this account
- Verification that you are licensed to collect in my state
- Your business license numbers and Registered Agent or Agent of Service

At this time I will also inform you that if your offices have reported invalidated information to any of the 3 major Credit Bureau's {Experian, Equifax or TransUnion} this action might constitute fraud under both Federal and State Laws. Due to this fact, if any negative mark is found on any of my credit reports by your company or the company that you represent, I will not hesitate to bring legal action against you for the following:

- Violation of the Fair Credit Reporting Act
- Violation of the Fair Debt Collection Practices Act
- Defamation of Character

If your offices are able to provide proper documentation as requested in the following Declaration, I will require at least 30 days to investigate this information and during such time all collection activity must cease and desist.

During this validation period, if any action is taken which could be considered detrimental to any of my credit reports, I will consult with my legal counsel for suit. This includes listing any information with a credit reporting repository that could be inaccurate or invalidated or verifying an account as accurate, when in fact there is no provided proof that it is accurate.

If your company fails to respond to this validation request within 30 days from the date of your receipt, all references to this account must be deleted and completely removed from my credit report and a copy of such deletion {to any/all of the 3 major credit reporting bureaus: Equifax, Experian and TransUnion} request shall be sent to me immediately.

I am formally requesting, in writing, that no telephone contact be made by your company to my home or my place of employment. If your office attempts telephone communication with me, including but not limited to computer generated calls and calls or correspondence sent to or with any third parties, it will be considered harassment and I will have no choice but to file suit. All future communications with me MUST be done in writing and sent to the address noted in this letter .

It would be advisable that you assure your records are in order before I am forced to take legal action against your company and your client. This is an attempt to correct your records, any information obtained shall be used for that purpose.

Best Regards,

LETTER OF GOODWILL – Sample

Dear Sirs,

I have been a GLADSTONES customer since 2011 and during that time, I have enjoyed my experience with GLADSTONES greatly. I am writing to see if you would be willing to make a "goodwill" adjustment to your reporting to the three credit agencies. I have two late payments on the above referenced account that date back to 2011. Since that time I have been an exceptional customer paying every month on time. Because of my exceptional payment history over the last X years, I would like you to consider removing the negative payments from my credit report. At the time of the late payments, I was in the process of changing jobs. I say that not to justify why the payments were late, but rather to show that the late payments are not a good indicator of my actual credit worthiness. I hope that GLADSTONES is willing to work with me on erasing this mark from my credit reports. I have been a very happy customer in the past and hope to continue a long relationship with GLADSTONES. With today's credit industry so competitive, I know how important it is to maintain good relationships with customers. GLADSTONES has been exceptional in my book so far and I highly recommend it to all my friends and relatives. I hope that you will deeply consider my request and prove once again, why GLADSTONES is heads above the rest. I look forward to your reply

HIPPA VIOLATION – Sample Letter

Account # xxxxx678

To Whom It May Concern:

Please be advised I have requested **VALIDATION** (not verification) of an item reported to you by the above original creditor/collection agency. I have received a response that does not indicate or prove:

1. That I had this service

2. The services for which I am being charged. OR

3. The cost of each service for which I am being charged.

Furthermore, Apex Collections did NOT provide me a HIPPA release that releases my medical information to them, therefore by providing such information they are in VIOLATION of my HIPPA rights. I am proceeding with legal action as prescribed by law against the above named original creditor/collection agency. Should this item not be deleted within the required time allowed by law I will seek every legal remedy available to me and file suit against the credit bureau responsible for reporting this violation.

I urge you to take this extremely seriously as I have documented my case without error. I encourage a response from you expeditiously. Thank you for your time and assistance.

86 The Credit Card Offers - Have you ever noticed that whenever your credit report gets accessed you start getting pre-approved credit card offers in the mail? To stop this you can include: Please add a Promotional Suppression to my credit file. That should do the trick!

APPENDIX I
How to Sue Creditors and Win Without a Lawyer

Most creditors DO NOT abide by the laws set by the Fair Credit Act and if they do you can still sue them. Some actions of a creditor that substantiate a law suit are: failure to validate a debt; calls you at work or very late at night; erroneous reporting of your credit history; and, refusing to note partial payments on your credit. Most of the time the creditors don't bother showing up, and why would they? If the debt is for $1,000 and they have to pay an attorney, travel fees and court fees they generally don't. Now if it's for a $25,000 credit card or maybe apartment you may not get so lucky but you can still win your case. If they don't show up you automatically win and receive a judgment of removal you can send to the (3) credit bureaus. By law the credit bureaus will now have to remove the debt from your credit report, whether it's valid or not. Also, see the HIPPA section below for medical debt.

- Get proof (most of the time you don't need it) but take screen shots of your phone or letter from your boss or even employee saying they called, copy of your credit report etc. You have to build a case against these people and it's generally very easy because the majority do not follow the laws outlined in the Fair Credit Act.

- Every state is different so you need to check what your state's maximum is for filing in small claims court. File your claim with the Small Claims court located in your county. Do not ever file for the state maximum for loss, always file it for a smaller amount. To file a claim, just go to the county courthouse and get the appropriate forms. Make sure to follow all the legal steps for filing this claim, including notifying the other party. Every state has different forms but they are all pretty self explanatory. Generally, there will be a section where you will insert your claim, make sure to ALWAYS include: REMOVAL OF DEROGATORY DEBT from all three credit bureaus; TransUnion, Experian and Equifax along with a dollar amount. This is super important. Without this you don't really gain anything.

- Once your claim is submitted you may have to notify the creditor or collection company. This is the easy part. Don't bother tracking them down too much, a lot of collection companies change addresses often. And it's in your advantage if they never receive it.

- Once the court hearing comes, the creditor or collection representative may or may not show up. Most often the creditor and or the collection company is not located in your county or even state. Like I said, they generally do not for smaller debt. If they do, make sure you have your facts strait and list what Fair Credit Act law they broke, which again is super easy because most don't follow the laws. Please see the document for the fair credit act laws. Now if they don't show up, you automatically win and the courts will give you your judgment (what you asked for).

- HIPPA laws are very strict. If you validated your debt and the collection agency provided a list of your debt from the hospital or doctor they violated your HIPPA rights. Your medical information can never be shared to a third party without your consent. Some doctors and hospitals are getting

44

smart about this and they bury the vernacular within forms you sign. Always read these forms and draw a line through anything that talks about sharing your information with a 3rd party. Winning a HIPPA case is super easy and most of the time they won't show because they know they broke the law.

Remember, suing a collection company or creditor is easy and you don't need an expensive attorney. The cost to benefit is usually exponential. If you have a debt that's hurting your score by 50 points or more and they keep validating this is honestly your last hope. I've seen cases over $10,000 that the creditor nor collection agency never showed and the debt was relieved, it can be that easy. Sure it's more work for you but to have an extra 50 points on your credit or better interest rate on your car or home it's worth it. Never give up fighting!

APPENDIX II
How to Remove a Tax Lien Judgement

Step 1: Complete IRS Form 12277 This form serves as a request for withdrawal of the original tax lien. Before filling out this form, try to locate the Form 668(Y) you were sent by the IRS as notification of the original tax lien. This can help to expedite the process. However, you can still fill out this form if you don't have the 668(Y). For questions 11 on the form, select the option that states: "The taxpayer, or the Taxpayer Advocate acting on behalf of the taxpayer, believes withdrawal is in the best interest of the taxpayer and the government." For question 12, enter the words "Fresh Start Program."

Step 2: Send Form 122277 to the IRS Use IRS publication 4235 to determine the regional IRS where your form should be mailed. Send your form via certified mail.

Step 3: Wait for response from IRS After 30-45 days, the IRS will contact the court house where the lien was filed to notify them to withdraw it. You will also be sent a copy of this notification.

Step 4: Dispute the lien with the Credit Reporting Agencies When you dispute a tax lien with Equifax, Experian or TransUnion, they contact the courthouse where the lien was filed to determine if the information is still accurate. Since the courthouse has been notified that your lien was withdrawn, by disputing the lien with the above Credit Reporting Agencies at their respective websites, you should be able to have the lien removed quickly.

Step 5: Final confirmation Each of the credit reporting agencies will send you a notification of how your dispute turned out. If the lien was not removed from any or all of your reports, file a second dispute in writing and include a copy of the notification from the IRS that your lien has been withdrawn. Tax liens on a credit report can not only bring down your credit score significantly, but they can also be a deciding factor in a lender deciding to deny you a loan or credit card. Getting them resolved and off your credit reports a quickly as possible is imperative. If you have unpaid liens, visit IRS.gov to learn more about your options for settlement or payment plan.

NOTES

Author's Note. For anyone who caught it, yes, "The Big Three" is infact a nod to the TV program THIS IS US.

www.ingramcontent.com/pod-product-compliance
Lightning Source LLC
Chambersburg PA
CBHW021929170526
45157CB00005B/2246